The Truly *Offal* Recipe Book
by Curtis Pritchard

All Rights Reserved. No part of this publication may be reproduced in any form or by any means, including scanning, photocopying, or otherwise without prior written permission of the copyright holder. Copyright © 2014

Contents

1. Introduction
2. Braised Stuffed Lambs Hearts
3. Lamb Hearts with Zingy Gremolata
4. Anticuchos (Peruvian Beef Heart Kebabs)
5. French StyleHearts Cooked in Red Wine
6. Pickled Venison Heart
7. Char-Grilled Venison Heart with Peppers and Onions
8. Devilish Devilled Kidneys
9. Yorkshire Style Steak & Kidney Pie
10. Andalucian Kidneys
11. Lamb's Kidney with Autumn Mushrooms
12. This Little Piggy's Kidney on Toast
13. The Best Chicken Liver Paté
14. Duck Liver Rob Roy
15. Uncle Stu's Sautéed Calf's Liver
16. Chicken Liver Chilli Challenge
17. Quinta dos Pila Peri-Peri Chicken Livers
18. Claret Braised Oxtail
19. Caribean Oxtail Stew
20. Chinese Braised Oxtail Stew
21. The Richest Oxtail Soup
22. Oxtail Stew with Dark Chocolate
23. Pauper's Braised Tongue
24. Crispy Cow Tongue
25. Fruity Beef Tongue
26. Festive Pickled Cow Tongue
27. Crispy Fried Cod Tongues

28. Hancock's Grilled Sweetbreads
29. Awesome Sweetbread Tacos
30. Chicken-Fried Sweetbread Bitess
31. Golden Brown Sweetbreads with Fennel Salad
32. Lancashire Tripe And Onions
33. Tripe Espana
34. Maxed Out Tripe
35. Simple Pig's Trotters
36. Pork Trotter Terrine with Gribiche Sauce
37. Goats Trotters Curry
38. Ye Olde Jellied Pigs Feet
39. Stornoway Style Black Pudding
40. Sanguinaccio Dolce (Sweet Blood Pudding)
41. Scandinavian Pig's Blood Rye Bread
42. Crispy Lambs' Brains
43. Beef Brain
44. Sheep's Brains en Matelote
45. Sister Mary's Rooster Combs and Testicles.
46. Pig's Ears with Sofrito
47. Zuppa di Polmone (Lung Soup)
48. Slow Roasted Marrow Bones
49. The Ultimate Rocky Mountain Oysters
50. Mother's Haggis

1. Introduction

Hi folks! First off I would like to thank you for picking up my book of Truly *Offal* Recipes. In this book I will show you how to cook up fantastic dishes from the more unusual parts of the animal that modern cookbooks rarely show you. You see, cooking with cows heart, lamb brains or calf testicles is something that many people shy away from. But why? These animal parts have been part of the human diet since we first chowed down on a woolly mammoth so it makes sense that these ingredients should be part of our diet today. In fact, when cooked right they are good for us, rich in minerals and nutrients for a healthy lifestyle, and to make it even better, offal is *really* cheap so good for our wallet too.
I hope you enjoy reading my book and trying out these recipes for yourself as much as I have eating them over the years.

~ Curtis Pritchard

Hearts ~ Easy to find as most butchers and supermarkets now stock them. They are very lean and can be quite tough so need a long slow cooking time. Common types are beef, lamb, pork and Chicken.

Kidneys ~ When properly prepared kidneys are delicious and very nutritious. They can become very tough and chewy if overcooked so test them as you go along. Their rich flavor adds body as well as texture to hearty stews and pies.

Liver ~ Rich in vitamin A and iron, liver is another strong flavoured organ which needs gentle cooking. It pairs exceptionally well with onions.

Oxtail ~ The tail of any cattle, not just an ox, it needs slow cooking to make the meat tender. It is intensely flavored which makes it ideal for stocks and soups.

Tongue ~ Getting more and more popular in the restaurant scene, this ingredient is quite challenging for some people to try, but cooked well in a rich sauce it is lovely... and very cheap.

Sweetbreads ~ What are they? They are an animal's pancreas and thymus glands which when cooked get crispy on the outside and stay creamy on the inside. Truly delicious and a real delicacy the top chefs are using these days.

Tripe ~ The stomach of an animal, usually a cow,pig or sheep. This is an acquired tasted but when cooked well with a rich onion sauce, this can be one of the cheapest and most nutritious ingredients in town

Brains ~ One of the more gruesome ingredients but the mild, sweet flavour is worth trying.

Testicles ~ The animal does not even have to die for us to get these. Used from castrated calf's these are brilliant when sautéed, or deep fried cowboy style.

2. Braised Stuffed Lambs Hearts

Ingredients:

4 lambs hearts
3/4 cup (50 g) fresh white breadcrumbs
Grated rind of half a small lemon
1 level tbsp chopped parsley
1/2 level tbsp chopped thyme
2 tbsp milk Salt and pepper
3 carrots, sliced
2 onions, chopped
2 sticks of celery, sliced
1 parsnip, diced
2 tbsp (1 oz) 25 g dripping (fat from roasted meat)
3/4 pt (450ml) water
1 beef bouillon cube (stock cube)
1 level tbsp cornflour

Method:

Wash the hearts thoroughly and leave to soak in salted water for 30 minutes. Use scissors or a sharp knife to remove the tubes.

Combine together all the stuffing ingredients in a bowl and use to fill the cavities in the hearts.

Heat the oven to 350F / 180C Gas Mark 4.

Place all the vegetables in the bottom of a 3 pt / 1.7 litre heatproof casserole dish.

Melt the dripping in a frying pan and fry the hearts lightly until brown on all sides. Remove from the pan and place on top of the vegetables.

Drain any dripping from the pan, then add the water and crumbled bouillon cube and bring to the boil, stirring until well mixed.

Pour into the casserole dish. Cover with a lid or foil and cook in the oven for about 1 3/4 hours or until the hearts are tender.

Lift out the hearts and arrange on a warm serving dish with the vegetables.

Blend the cornflour with some cold water and stir into the casserole until the sauce thickens.

Place back in the oven for 2-3 minutes to cook, then pour the sauce over the hearts.

Serve.

3. Lamb Hearts with Zingy Gremolata

Ingredients:

4 lamb's hearts
1 tbsp Plain flour
2 tbsp vegetable oil or non-virgin olive oil
600g root vegetables (carrots, parsnips, artichokes etc) chopped into large chunks
Glass of red wine
600ml chicken stock
250g salad potatoes
6 cloves garlic, roughly chopped
3 Bay leaves
Stalks of parsley and thyme, tied into a bouquet garni
Salt & pepper

Gremolata Ingredients:

Grated zest of one lemon
1 tablespoon lemon juice
1 clove garlic, finely chopped
Handful chopped mixed fresh thyme, rosemary and parsley

Method:

Prepare the hearts by simply cutting out the tubes that pop out the top of the hearts or ask your butcher tho do this for you.

Preheat the oven to 110C / 230F. Roll the hearts in flour. Take a heavy-bottomed casserole dish, add the oil and put it onto a high heat until smoking hot.

Lightly brown the hearts in the oil, turning to sear them all around for about 6 minutes. Remove the hearts and set aside, then add the prepared root vegetables to the pan and fry for 5 minutes.

Season with salt and pepper and add everything else except the gremolata ingredients and turn up the heat.

When it starts to simmer, put the lid on and transfer it to the oven. Braise it for a minimum of 1 ½ hours (max 3hrs), a long slow cook the best.

Prepare the gremolata ingredients and set aside in a bowl.

Remove from the oven and remove the bouquet garni. Using a slotted spoon, decant all the meat and vegetables to another bowl, leaving all the juices behind. Boil the juices for about 5-10 minutes until they have reduced to a good thick gravy.

Scatter the gremolata on the hearts and serve with creamy mash potatoes.

4. Anticuchos (Peruvian Beef Heart Kebabs)

Ingredients:

1 tbsp vegetable oil
1 red chili, chopped
2 tsp ground cumin
1 crushed clove of garlic
4 tbsp vinegar
750g/1lb trimmed beef heart (about half a medium heart) cut into matchbox-size pieces
4 tomatoes, chopped
4 spring onions, chopped
Half a lime
1kg/2.2lb sweet potatoes, baked in their jackets until soft

Method:

Mix the oil, chili, cumin, garlic, vinegar and beef heart with half a teaspoonful of salt and a good grind of black pepper.

Cover and rest in the fridge for at least a couple of hours or overnight.

Thread the meat on to skewers. Heat a griddle pan or grill until extremely hot.

Cook the meat for about 3-4 minutes on each side until well charred (this adds the right smoky flavour). Leave to rest for 10 minutes or so before eating.

Mix the tomato, spring onion and a squeeze of lime juice to make the salsa. Season with salt and pepper.

Serve the anticuchos with the tomato salsa and the sweet potatoes.

5. French Style Hearts in Red Wine

Ingredients:

4 lamb or sheep hearts
100 ml table vinegar
2 sprigs fresh thyme (or 1 tsp dried)
4 garlic cloves, finely chopped
3 laurel leaves
salt and pepper
100 g butter
100 g smoked bacon, finely chopped
10-15 shallots, sliced
1-2 tbsp flour
400-500 ml red wine
100-200 ml water
salt and pepper
200 g whole small mushrooms, sautéed

Cut the fat off the hearts, rinse them well under running cold water and cut lengthwise into four parts.

Mix the vinegar, thyme, garlic and laurel to make the marinade and season well with salt and pepper.
Marinade the heart pieces for 4-6 hours.

Melt the butter in a deep frying pan. Remove the hearts from the marinade and brown in the butter.

Add the bacon and onions. Sprinkle the sifted flour into the pan and mix with the butter. Add red wine and water and mix well. Season with salt and pepper.

Simmer until the hearts are cooked, about 1 to 1 1/2 hours.
Add the sautéed mushrooms and season to taste if necessary.
Serve with boiled potatoes and green beans.

6. Pickled Venison Heart

Ingredients:

1 venison heart
1/2 ts brown sugar
3 small white onions
1/3 qt cold water
1/2 ts salt
1/2 ts black pepper
white cider vinegar

Method:

Boil the venison heart in enough water to cover.

When water starts to boil add the brown sugar and boil for 30 to 45 minutes until nicely cooked. Drain heart and cool in refrigerator.

When cool dice the heart into chunks.

Slice the onions and mix with the meat and place in clean jar. Half fill the jar with cold water and season with salt and pepper.

Finish filling jar with white cider vinegar. Seal the jar with the cap and shake the jar so all the ingredients mix well.

Place in the refrigerator for a few days before eating.

7. Grilled Venison Heart with Peppers and Onions

Ingredients:

1-2 deer hearts, or 1 elk, moose or beef heart
4 tablespoons olive oil, divided
1 tablespoon sherry or red wine vinegar
1 tablespoon Worcestershire sauce
1 teaspoon salt
1 teaspoon dried oregano
1 teaspoon dried thyme
1 teaspoon ground black pepper
3-4 colored bell peppers, cut into 2-3 pieces each
1 large onion, cut into large wedges

Method:

Trim the hearts. Mix 2 tablespoons of olive oil with the vinegar, Worcestershire sauce, salt, oregano, thyme and black pepper in a large bowl. Massage the marinade into the meat, put everything into a container and marinade for 6-8 hours.

Heat the grill.

Coat the peppers and onion in the rest of the olive oil and salt well.

Grill everything on high heat. Put the hearts and vegetables on the grill, skin side down for the peppers, and leave them alone with the grill cover open for 8 minutes. Flip everything and grill, uncovered, for 5 more minutes.

Check the peppers and onions, and when they are nicely cooked with a little char, remove and put in foil to steam.

Remove any blackened skin from the peppers.

When the hearts are cooked tent the hearts loosely with foil and let rest for 5-10 minutes.

Sprinkle with salt and pepper and serve with the vegetables.

8. Devilish Devilled Kidneys

Ingredients:

(serves two)

4 lamb's kidneys, skinned, cored and diced
1 heaped tsp of flour
salt
cayenne pepper
1 tbsp dry English mustard
25g butter
1 tsp of Worcestershire sauce
75ml chicken stock
2 pieces of hot buttered toast

Dust the kidneys with flour, salt and plenty of cayenne pepper then roll them in the dry mustard powder.

Melt the butter in a small frying pan and cook the kidneys over a gentle heat for five minutes, turning them now and again. They should be just pink inside.

When they are almost done to your liking, pour the Worcestershire sauce and the stock around them, simmer until the gravy is thick and serve them on hot buttered toast.

9. Yorkshire Style Steak & Kidney Pie

Ingredients:

880g Steak and Kidney
1 tsp Salt
½ tsp Pepper
2 tbsp Plain Flour
4-6 tbsp Olive Oil
1 Onion (chopped)
125g Button Mushrooms
1 tbsp Tomato Puree
400 ml Guinness or Milk Stout
2 Bay Leaves
4 sprigs Thyme
200 ml Beef Stock
500g Puff Pastry
1 Egg Yolk

Method:

Preheat the oven to 160C /320F / Gas Mark 2.

Place the steak and kidney in a plastic bag with the salt, pepper and flour. Seal the bag and shake well until the meat is thoroughly coated.

Heat 2 to 3 tbsp oil in casserole dish over a high heat; sear the meat all over in the hot oil in 2-3 batches, adding more oil each time.

Remove with a slotted spoon and leave set aside. Add the onions and mushrooms to the casserole and cook for 2-3 minutes. Add the tomato puree and cook for a further 2-3 minutes.

Deglaze with the Guinness then add bay leaves, thyme, steak and kidney and stock. Bring to the boil then cover and place in the oven for 1½ hours.

Take the casserole out of oven and place on the hob. Reduce the sauce over a medium heat to a smooth, gravy like consistency and allow to cool.

To complete the cooking, preheat the oven to 180C/360F/Gas mark 4. Place the steak and kidney from the casserole into a 1 litre pie dish and brush the pie rim with egg yolk. Roll out the pastry to 5 mm thick and place on top of the pie dish, carefully pressing down the rim. Brush the pastry with the remaining egg yolk and bake in the middle of the oven for 35-40 minutes.

Serve with creamy mashed potatoes, garden peas and carrots.

10. Andalucian Kidneys

Ingredients:

serves 4

8 - 10 lambs' kidneys
50 g (2 oz) butter
1 medium-sized onion, finely chopped
6 - 8 button mushrooms, thinly sliced
25 g (1 oz) flour
300 ml (10 fl oz) hot chicken stock
30 - 45 ml (2 - 3 tbsp) dry sherry
salt and freshly ground black pepper
4 slices of bread, crusts removed
olive oil for frying
15 - 30 ml (1 - 2 tbsp) freshly chopped parsley

Method:

Skin and halve the kidneys, removing the core. In a small frying-pan heat half the butter. Sauté the kidneys for 2-3 minutes. Remove with a slotted spoon and put aside.

Cook the onion in the remaining butter until soft and lightly browned. Add the thinly sliced mushrooms and cook, stirring continuously, until lightly coloured. Remove from the heat.

Return the kidneys to the pan. Sprinkle with the flour and combine carefully. Stir in the hot chicken stock and return the pan to the heat. Bring to the boil, reduce the heat and simmer for 5 minutes. . Add the sherry, and season with salt and freshly ground black pepper to taste.

Meanwhile, cut the slices of bread into triangles. Heat the olive oil and fry the croutons until golden brown. Remove from the oil, drain on absorbent paper and keep warm.

To serve, transfer the kidneys to a heated serving dish. Dip the edges of the croutons in parsley and arrange around the edge of the dish, sprinkle the remaining chopped parsley over the kidneys and serve immediately.

11. Lamb's Kidney with Autumn Mushrooms.

Ingredients:

2 large or 3 small lamb's kidneys
3 tbsp extra-virgin olive oil
100g mixed autumn mushrooms, sliced
1 tbsp roughly chopped fresh tarragon
1 tsp pink peppercorns
4 handfuls of a selection of lettuce and rocket leaves

For the dressing
1½ tbsp extra-virgin olive oil
½ tbsp white wine vinegar
1 tsp Dijon mustard

Method:

Combine the dressing ingredients together in a small bowl or jar, season and set aside.

Prepare the kidneys by removing the fatty membrane from the centre of the kidneys with a sharp knife, then cut into 1-2cm cubes.

Heat 2 tbsp of the olive oil in a frying pan over a medium-high heat. Add the autumn mushrooms, season and cook, stirring frequently for 2-3 minutes. Stir in the tarragon, then remove to a plate.

Add the rest of the olive oil to the pan and, when hot, add the kidneys. Season, then cook, stirring occasionally, for 2-3 minutes until golden brown on the outside but still slightly pink in the centre. Add the pink peppercorns for the last few seconds, then remove everything to the plate with the mushrooms.

Toss the salad leaves in just enough dressing to lightly coat, then divide among plates. Spoon over the mushrooms and kidneys, then serve immediately.

12. This Little Piggy's Kidney on Toast

Ingredients:

1 pig's kidney
olive oil, for frying
about 1 tbsp butter
1 thick slice bread, preferably sourdough
1 small banana shallot, finely chopped
1 splash white wine vinegar
1 tsp wholegrain mustard
1 tsp crème fraîche

Method:

Soak two wooden skewers in water for at least 10 minutes.

Butterfly the kidney by slicing through it horizontally with a sharp knife without fully cutting it in half. Open it like a book and cut out the white tendons. Wash in cold water and peel off the outer membrane. Season well with salt and pepper.

Skewer the kidney open using the two soaked skewers.

Heat a splah of oil in a frying pan and fry the kidney for 1-2 minutes on each side, until browned. Add a knob of butter to the pan as you turn the kidney over.

On a griddle, toast the bread with a little olive oil.

Once the kidney is cooked, remove from the pan and leave to rest. Add the shallot to the pan and fry until softened. Add a splash of vinegar and cook until all the liquid has been absorbed.

Stir in the mustard. Add the crème fraîche and mix again. Return the kidney to the pan and cook in the sauce for 1-2 minutes, spooning the sauce over the meat.

To serve, top the hot toast with the kidney and drizzle the sauce over the top.

13. The Best Chicken Liver Paté

Ingredients:

1 pound fresh chicken livers, cleaned
1 cup milk
1 stick cold unsalted butter, cut into pieces
1 cup chopped yellow onions
2 teaspoons minced garlic
2 tablespoons green peppercorns, drained
2 bay leaves
1 teaspoon chopped fresh thyme leaves
1/2 teaspoon salt
1/2 teaspoon freshly ground black pepper
1/4 cup Cognac or brandy
Chopped parsley leaves, for garnish
French bread croutons or toasted brioche

Method:

In a bowl, soak the livers in the milk for 2 hours. Drain well.

In a large sauté pan or skillet, melt 4 tablespoons of the butter over medium-high heat. Add the onions and cook, stirring, until soft, about 3 minutes. Add the garlic and cook until it releases its aromas, about 30 seconds.

Add the chicken livers, 1 tablespoon of the peppercorns, the bay leaves, thyme, salt, and pepper and cook, stirring, until the livers are browned on the outside and still slightly pink on the inside, about 5 minutes.

Add the Brandy and cook until most of the liquid is evaporated and the livers are cooked through but still tender.

Remove from the heat cool slightly. Remove the bay leaves.

In a food processor, blend the liver mixture. Add the remaining butter in pieces and pulse until smooth.

Fold in the remaining 1 tablespoon peppercorns and adjust the seasoning, to taste.

Pack the paté into 6 individual ramekins or small molds. Cover with plastic and refrigerate until firm, at least 6 hours.

To serve, place the ramekins on individual plates. Garnish the tops with parsley and surround with croutons, toasted brioche, green salad and balsamic dressing.

14. Duck Liver Rob Roy

Ingredients:

400g of duck livers
salt
vegetable oil
20g of butter
2 shallots, finely diced
50ml of whisky
120ml of brown Chicken stock
75g of double cream
2 tbsp of chopped parsley
2 tbsp of chopped chives
1 dash of lemon juice
1 knob of butter
1 loaf of brioche, 4 thick slices

Method:

Clean the duck livers.

Add vegetable oil to lightly coat the base of a frying pan and place on a high heat. Sauté the duck livers until golden brown on both sides, season with salt, remove from the pan and rest in a warm place.

Add the butter to the same pan with the shallots and sweat until soft. Add whisky and reduce until almost most of the liquid has evaporated.

Add chicken stock and again reduce by half.

Finish the whisky sauce with double cream and reduce sauce until it thickens slightly to the right consistency. Season with salt to taste and leave in a warm place.

For the brioche, trim off the crusts and cut to a desirable shape. Heat a large knob of butter in a frying pan and fry slices of brioche in butter until golden brown, remove from the pan and place on absorbent kitchen towel to absorb any excess fat.

To serve the livers, reheat the sauce and add the chives, parsley and a dash of lemon juice. Place the warm livers on the toasted brioche and sauce generously. The livers should be slightly pink in the middle.

15. Uncle Stu's Sautéed Calf's Liver

Ingredients:

1 pound calf's liver, cut into 1/2 inch thick pieces
1 1/2 cups whole milk
4 tablespoons unsalted butter
2 medium onions, thinly sliced
1/2 cup all-purpose flour
Coarse salt and freshly ground pepper
2 tablespoons sunflower or other neutral-tasting oil, plus more as needed
4 fresh sage sprigs, thinly sliced

Method:

Place liver in a ceramic bowl and pour milk over. Refrigerate, covered for 5 to 6 hours.

In a large skillet, heat 2 tablespoons butter over medium-high heat. When butter is shimmering, add onions. Cook, stirring occasionally, until softened and translucent for 5 to 10 minutes. Reduce heat to medium-low and continue to cook, stirring more frequently until onions are very soft and brown, 30 to 40 minutes more.

Drain liver and throw away the milk. Pat liver dry with paper towels.

Spread flour on a plate and season with salt and pepper. Thoroughly coat liver with the flour mixture, shaking off any excess.

Heat a large (13-inch) sauté pan over medium heat and add remaining 2 tablespoons butter and the oil and heat until shimmering. Cook (in batches, if necessary, to avoid crowding pan) until liver is firm (but not hard) and browned on the outside but still slightly pink in the centre, 1 to 2 minutes per side. Repeat with remaining liver, adding more oil to the pan as necessary.

Add sage and cook for 1 minute more.

Divide liver among plates and top with onions.

16. Chicken Liver Chilli Challenge.

Ingredients:

1 lb / 450 grams Chicken livers
4 shallots (chopped finely)
1/2 Tomato (chopped finely)
1.5 tsp Ginger Garlic paste
1.5 tsp cumin powder
Pinch of Chilli powder
Turmeric powder
Cumin seeds
Salt to taste 1.5 tbsp
Coriander leaves

Method:

Wash chicken liver.

Add turmeric powder and soak for a couple of minutes.

Drain the water and leave the chicken on a kitchen towel.

Add 1.5 tbsp of oil in a pan. When it is hot, add cumin seeds and fry for a few seconds.
Add chopped onions and sauté for a until soft.

Add turmeric powder and let it blend with the onions. Before it turns golden brown, add the chopped tomatoes and toss them for a minute or until they softens. Sprinkling salt at this stage helps cook the dish quickly.

Add 1.5 tsp of ginger-garlic paste and mix it well until the raw smell disappears.
Add the chicken liver, cut into small cubes (3 x 3 cm).

Mix and toss it until the colour changes (2 minutes approximately).

Add chilli powder, pepper powder, cumin powder (optional) and salt. Mix it with the chicken liver.

Add 4 tbsp of water and let it cook until the water evaporates.

Keep tossing until you see the oil leaving the pan (in small amounts). Garnish with coriander leaves and serve with hot rice.

17. Quinta dos Pila Peri-Peri Chicken Livers

Ingredients:

1 onion, thinly slices
1/4 teaspoon ground cloves
1/2 teaspoon ground cumin
olive oil and butter for frying
1kg ripe tomatoes
2 cloves of garlic, crushed
1 teaspoon ground peri-peri chili (you can also add fresh chili, finely chopped)
1/2 teaspoon smoked paprika
peri-peri sauce for extra heat
500g free range chicken livers
100ml Madeira or similar fortified wine or even brandy
100ml cream (optional)
flat leaf parsley
sea salt and black pepper to taste
Portuguese rolls to serve

Method:

Cook the onions first until soft and caramelised. Melt some butter and olive oil in a saucepan, add the sliced onions and cook on a medium to low heat until golden brown.
Set aside.

Blanche the tomatoes in simmering water. Peel the skin from the tomatoes, then cut in half and half again. Remove the seeds, dice roughly and set aside.

Using a pestle and mortar create a paste from the ground chili, fresh chili, paprika and garlic. Add some olive oil to a medium size saucepan, add the paste and fry for 1 minute. Add the chopped tomatoes and cook for a further 5 minutes.

At this stage add your hot sauce to your liking. Allow the sauce to simmer on a low heat whilst you prepare the rolls and cook the livers.

Cut a hollow in each Portuguese roll. Toast under the grill.

To finish off, add the cream as well as the peri-peri tomato sauce, stirring to combine. Add the freshly chopped parsley. Spoon into the bread bowls, pop on the lids and serve.

18. Claret Braised Oxtail

Ingredients:
2 kg oxtail pieces
4 tbsp plain flour, seasoned with salt and pepper
4 tbsp olive oil
2 red onions, finely sliced
2 celery sticks, finely chopped
1 carrot, finely chopped
2 tbsp tomato purée
375ml (half a bottle) good Claret
300ml beef stock, hot
Good grating of fresh nutmeg
1 tbsp plain flour
1 tbsp butter, softened

Method:

Dust the oxtail in the flour until lightly coated. Heat half the oil in a heavy-based casserole with a tight-fitting lid. Fry the oxtail, in batches, over a medium heat, for 2-3 minutes each side until browned. Drain off and discard the excess fat. Set aside.

Heat the remaining oil in the casserole and gently fry the onion, celery and carrot for 10 minutes until lightly golden.

Stir in the tomato purée, then return the oxtail to the casserole. Pour in the Claret and stock. Add the nutmeg, season with salt and black pepper, then bring to the boil.

Cover with the lid, reduce the heat to low and simmer for 2½-3 hours until the oxtail is tender. Take the oxtail out of the pot, set aside and keep warm. Remove the solids from the pot with a slotted spoon, then bring the sauce to a vigorous boil and bubble until reduced by half. Mix the flour and butter in a bowl to make a beurre manié. Gradually whisk a little at a time into the sauce. Bubble for 3-5 minutes until thickened.
Return the oxtail and solids to the pot to warm through. Serve with baked potatoes or creamy mashed potato and seasonal vegetables.

19. Caribbean Oxtail Stew

Ingredients:

3lbs Oxtail
1 1/2 tsp Salt
1 tsp Black pepper
3 Tbsp curry powder
2 Cloves garlic
2 Tbsp Cooking oil
2 Medium onions, sliced
1 tsp Dried thyme (or 1 Tbsp fresh thyme leaves)
1 Tbsp hot pepper sauce
2 Tbsp Tomato ketchup
1 tsp Worcestershire sauce
3 cups Water
1 Can (19oz) Lima beans (also called butter beans), drain and set aside liquid

Method:

Season oxtail with salt, black pepper, 2 Tbsp curry powder and garlic.

Place sliced onions on top, cover and place in refrigerator overnight or for at least for 2 hours before cooking.

While heating oil in heavy saucepan remove onions from top of meat.

Add oxtail to the sauce pan and sear to seal in juice.

Add 1 cup of water, thyme and onion. stir. Stir in hot pepper sauce, tomato ketchup and Worcestershire sauce; cook for 5 minutes.

Add 1 Tbsp curry powder; stir. Add 2 cups of water (enough water to just cover meat); cover and simmer until meat is tender (2 to 2 1/2 hours). The meat should be so tender it's falling off the bone.

Add lima beans (with half their liquid) to the cooked meat and stir.

Raise heat and bring to a rapid boil until gravy thickens, stirring at intervals so that no sticking or burning occurs.

Remove from heat.

Serve with steamed white rice and a mixed green salad

20. Chinese Braised Oxtail Stew

Ingredients:

5 to 6 pounds oxtails, cut into pieces, fat trimmed
Salt and ground black pepper
2 to 4 tablespoons vegetable oil
½ cup rice wine or dry sherry
2 cups low-sodium beef or chicken stock
1/3 cup dark or regular soy sauce
1½ tablespoons brown sugar
2 star anise, broken into pieces
2 whole cloves
4 lemongrass stalks, trimmed and bruised
3 scallions, trimmed and cut into 2-inch lengths, plus 2 scallions, thinly sliced on the diagonal, for garnish
6 slices fresh ginger
4 garlic cloves, peeled
3-4 Thai chili peppers, cut into 1/2-inch lengths
10 ounces fresh or dried whole shiitake mushrooms, stems removed, re-hydrated if dried
1 lime, zested and cut into small wedges

Method:

Heat oven to 150C / 300F. Season oxtails with salt and pepper. Heat 2 tablespoons oil in a large ovenproof pot with a tight-fitting lid. Working in batches if necessary to avoid crowding, brown oxtail all over. Add oil as needed.

When done browning, get rid of the extra fat from bottom of empty pot and set pot over high heat. Add the wine and bring to a boil, agitating browned bits. In a bowl, mix soy sauce and sugar with 2 cups stock and pour into pot. Add the lemongrass, chili peppers, star anise, cloves, 2-inch pieces of scallions, ginger and garlic and bring to a boil. Turn off heat. Return oxtails to pot and add lime zest. Cover and transfer to oven. Cook 1½ hours.

Turn over pieces of oxtail, cover again and cook 1½ hours more, or until oxtail is very tender. Remove oxtails from pot and strain sauce into a separate saucepan; discard contents of strainer. Transfer oxtail pieces back to ovenproof pot. Cover oxtails and sauce and refrigerate overnight.

The next day, heat oven to 300 degrees; remove oxtails and sauce from refrigerator. Lift off any fat on surface of sauce and discard. Gently warm sauce until liquid, then pour over oxtails and stir in shiitake mushrooms. Cover with foil or a lid and bake 30 minutes.

Uncover, stir and raise oven temperature to 200C / 400F. Cook, uncovered, 15 minutes. Stir again and cook another 15 minutes, until hot and glazed thickly with sauce. Remove oxtails from oven and serve over rice. Sprinkle each serving with thin scallion slices and squeeze lime juice over oxtails.

21. The Richest Oxtail Soup

Ingredients:
70g butter
1.5kg oxtail, cut into pieces and trimmed of excess fat
2 celery stalks, sliced
1 onion, stuck with 3 cloves
2 carrots, sliced
1 small turnip, peeled, quartered and sliced
1 leek, roughly chopped
1 bouquet garni (made up of a bay leaf, a couple of sprigs of thyme and three or four parsley stalks tied together with kitchen string)
10 black peppercorns
300ml red wine
Salt and freshly ground black pepper
60-80ml sherry
3 tbsp finely chopped parsley

Method:

Warm the butter in a large saucepan over medium heat and brown the oxtail pieces, in batches if necessary, until browned on all sides. Remove from the pan, set aside and sweat the vegetables in the meat juices for five minutes.

Return the meat to the pan, along with the bouquet garni, peppercorns, wine and one and a half to two litres of water. Season, bring to a boil and simmer, covered, until the meat is very tender and just about falling off the bones – about three to four hours.

Strain the liquid into a bowl, cool and refrigerate. Discard the veg, peppercorns and bouquet garni. Pull the meat from the bones, discarding any skin and fat. Place in a bowl, season and refrigerate.

Next day, remove the solid layer of fat that will have formed on the top of the stock, pour the stock into a pan, add the meat and bring just to a simmer. Adjust the seasoning to taste, add the sherry and simmer very gently for five minutes. Serve in warmed bowls, scattered with parsley

22. Oxtail Stew with Dark Chocolate

Ingredients:

4 pounds (2 kg) oxtail
salt, pepper
2-3 tablespoons olive oil
1 small piece of bacon or pancetta, chopped
1 onion, sliced
2 cloves garlic, finely chopped
1 carrot, sliced
¼ teaspoon ground cloves
¼ teaspoon ground cinnamon
1 cup (2.4 dl) wine, white or red
1 bay leaf
28 oz (800 g) canned tomatoes
5 cellary stalks, chopped
2 tablespoons raisins
Celery leaves, chopped
1 oz (30 g) bittersweet chocolate (75% cacao minimum)
2 tablespoons pine nuts

Method:
Season the oxtails with salt and pepper, and brown them well on all sides in olive oil.

Add bacon or pancetta, chopped onion, and garlic, and fry for a few minutes at medium heat.

Add carrot, wine, tomatoes, spices; cover the casserole, and cook for 4-5 hours at low heat until the meat is tender and almost falling off the bones.

Add water if necessary during cooking; the meat should be almost completely covered with liquid during cooking.

Take the casserole from the oven, and remove most of the fat from the surface of the sauce.
Add chopped celery stalks and raisins, make the final seasoning with salt and pepper to taste.
Cook for about 30-45 min more.

Add chopped celery leaves and chocolate, and mix well when the chocolate has melted. Sprinkle with pine nuts.

Serve with rice or polenta, or simply with good Italian bread to soak up all the sauce.

23. Pauper's Braised Tongue

Ingredients:

1 tongue, soaked and drained
3 Tbsp butter
3 Tbsp olive oil
2 onions, thinly sliced
3 carrots, sliced
3/4 cup dry white wine
9 ounces canned tomatoes
salt & pepper

Method:

Parboil the tongue in salted, boiling water for 20 minutes, then drain and skin the top of the tongue. Meanwhile, heat the butter and oil in a pan, add the onions and carrots and cook over low heat, stirring occasionally, for 5 minutes.

Add the tongue, cover and cook for 2 minutes more.

Mash the tomatoes with their juices in a bowl, add to the pan, cover and simmer for about 1 1/2 hours until the tongue is tender.

Remove the tongue from the pan. Ladle the cooking juices into a food processor or use a hand held blender to puree sauce. Reheat the sauce for a few minutes.

Slice the tongue, place on a warm serving dish and spoon the hot sauce over it.

24. Crispy Cow Tongue

Ingredients:

1 1/2 pounds beef, veal, or pork tongue (about 1 beef tongue or 2 to 3 pork tongues)
2 quarts chicken stock (or water)
olive oil, for brushing on tongue before grilling
Salt and freshly ground black pepper

Method:

Place the tongue(s) in a pot and cover with stock or water. Bring to a boil, reduce to a simmer, then cover and cook until tender, about three hours, adding extra liquid as needed.

Let the tongue cool, then remove the tongue from the stock and set the stock aside for another use.

When tongue is cool enough to handle, peel the outer membrane off the tongue and discard. Cut the tongue into 3/4-inch slices. Season with salt.

Brush the slices of tongue with olive oil. Grill until tongue is brown and a little crispy on the surface, then flip and grill on the other side, 10 to 15 minutes total. Remove from grill and serve with your choice of garnishes and seasonings.

25. Fruity Beef Tongue

Ingredients:

1 beef tongue (4 pounds)
2 onions
2 carrots, sliced
1 stick celery (with leaves), sliced
1 clove garlic, crushed
2 tablespoons butter
1/3 cup raisins
3 tablespoons almonds, chopped
1/3 cup white wine vinegar
1 tablespoon tomato paste
1/3 cup Madeira wine
2/3 cup tongue cooking broth
Salt and pepper to taste

Method:

Simmer the tongue in water to cover with one onion, coarsely chopped, the carrots, celery and garlic, for about three hours or until tender. Turn off heat and leave the tongue in its cooking broth while you prepare the sauce.

Chop the remaining onion and sauté in the butter in a small pan. Add the raisins and the almonds and fry until the almonds are golden brown.

Stir in the vinegar and tomato paste, then add the Madeira and stock. Simmer for three minutes to reduce slightly, season with salt and pepper to taste and keep warm.

Peel the tongue and slice it. Arrange the slices on a serving platter and pour the sauce over the top.

26. Festive Pickled Cow Tongue

Ingredients:

1 (about 3 pounds) fresh beef tongue
Salt
1 1/2 cups vinegar
2 cups granulated sugar
1/2 teaspoon whole cloves
2 teaspoons allspice
1 bay leaf
1 stick cinnamon
1/4 teaspoon ground pepper

Method:

Cover tongue with water. Add 1 teaspoon salt for each quart of water. Cover tightly and cook slowly until tender, about 2 1/2 to 3 hours.

When tongue is tender, remove the skin and cut away the roots. Plunging the tongue into cold water after cooking helps to loosen the skin.

Slice tongue crosswise about 1/8-inch thick.

Drain all but 2 cups of the water from pan. Add the remaining ingredients and return sliced meat to pan. Simmer, covered, for 1 hour. If the tongue is to be served cold, it will be more juicy if cooled in the liquid in which it is cooked. The cooling should be done under refrigeration or where there is circulation of cool air.

27. Crispy Fried Cod Tongues

Ingredients:

2 lbs fresh cod tongues, washed and dried
1 cup flour, season with 1 tsp salt and 1/2 tsp pepper
4 ounces of salt pork cut into small 1/4 inch cubes
2 Tbsp vegetable oil

Method:

Wash the cod tongues and dry with paper towels. Toss in the seasoned flour until lightly coated.

Cook the salt pork in a skillet over a medium until the pork pieces are crispy and have released or rendered their fat.

Add the vegetable oil to the skillet. Fry the cod tongues over medium-high heat until crispy and golden brown on each side.

Eat them plain or dip them in this simple, tangy tartare sauce.

Tartare Sauce:

2 egg yolks
Generous pinch of salt
1 tsp Dijon mustard
125ml sunflower or groundnut oil
125ml olive oil
2-3 tbsp pickling liquor from cornichons, to taste
1 heaped tbsp salted capers, rinsed and chopped
1 heaped tbsp cornichons, chopped
1 heaped tbsp chopped parsley
½ tbsp chopped chives

Mix the egg yolks, salt and mustard together in a food processor, or with electric beaters, or a whisk. Once well combined, very gradually drip in the oil, beating all the while, until you have mayonnaise – don't be tempted to add it too fast, especially near the beginning, or it will curdle. It will be very thick at the end, but don't worry, the pickling liquor will thin it down.

Stir in the pickling liquor, followed by the remaining ingredients. Taste and see if it needs seasoning, or indeed any extra pickle juice. Serve at room temperature.

28. Hancock's Grilled Sweetbreads

Ingredients:

1 lb sweetbreads
1 gallon cold water
1 cup distilled white vinegar
2 tablespoons salt
2 tablespoons extra-virgin olive oil
4 (12-inch) wooden skewers, soaked in warm water 1 hour

Method:

Rinse sweetbreads well, then transfer to a 6-quart pot and add water, vinegar, and salt. Bring to a boil over high heat, then reduce heat and simmer gently 10 minutes.

Drain sweetbreads in a colander, then transfer to a bowl of ice and cold water to cool.

While sweetbreads are cooling, prepare grill for cooking over direct heat with medium-hot charcoal or regular grill.

Drain sweetbreads, then pat dry gently and separate into roughly 1 1/2-inch pieces (about 20) using your fingers.

Toss sweetbread pieces with oil in a bowl, then thread onto skewers (about 5 pieces on each). Season with salt and pepper.

Grill sweetbreads on lightly oiled grill rack (covered only if using a gas grill), turning occasionally, until golden brown,

5 to 7 minutes total. Transfer to a platter and let stand, loosely covered with foil, 5 minutes.

29. Awesome Sweedbread Tacos

Ingredients:

1 pound veal sweetbreads
1 cup buttermilk
1 jalapeño sliced
1 clove garlic, minced
1/2 teaspoon ground cumin
1 cup all-purpose flour
1/2 teaspoon kosher salt, plus more to taste
1/2 teaspoon black pepper, plus more to taste
Pinch of cayenne
2 tablespoons unsalted butter
Warm tortillas, pico de gallo and sour cream for serving

Method:

Place the sweetbreads in a sealable container, cover with cold water, and soak for at least 2 hours.

Discard the soaking water and place the sweetbreads into a pot large enough to hold them. Cover with cold water and bring to a boil. Allow the sweetbreads to cook until they are white and puffy, about 5 minutes.

Drain sweetbreads in a colander and then place in a bowl with ice water to stop them from cooking.

Take the cooked sweetbreads and pat dry with a paper towel. You'll see a thin membrane, which you need to peel off of the meat. Chop off any gristly bits and then chop the sweetbreads into 1-inch sized pieces.

In a sealable container, place the chopped and cleaned sweetbreads and cover with the buttermilk, jalapeño, garlic and cumin.

Soak for at least 2 hours. Drain and rinse the sweetbreads. Mix together the flour, salt, black pepper and cayenne.

Taste and adjust seasonings. Lightly sprinkle the sweetbreads with salt and pepper and then dredge into the flour.

In a large skillet on medium low, heat up the butter. Add the floured sweetbreads and cook on each side until lightly browned and crisp, about 5 minutes.

Serve with warm tortillas, pico de gallo and sour cream.

30. Chicken-Fried Sweetbread Bites

Ingredients:

1 lb sweetbreads, lightly rinsed and cut into 1-inch chunks
2 cups milk
1/2 teaspoon salt
1 1/2 cup all purpose flour
1 tablespoon smoked paprika
2 teaspoons garlic powder
1 1/2 teaspoons onion powder
2 eggs, lightly beaten
salt and pepper to taste
grilled banana ketchup

Honey-mustard dipping sauce:

1/3 cup mayonnaise
1/4 cup honey
3 tablespoons whole grain mustard
1/8 teaspoon cayenne pepper
salt and pepper to taste
vegetable oil for frying

Directions:

Place sweetbreads, milk and salt into a bowl and stir together. Cover and place in the refrigerator overnight.

For honey-mustard: Place all ingredients into a bowl and stir together. Season with salt and pepper, cover and refrigerate for at least 6 hours.

Preheat oil to 175C / 350F.

Strain sweetbreads and gently rinse under cold water. Pat dry and set aside.

Place flour, paprika, garlic powder, and onion powder in a shallow dish and mix together.

Dip pieces of sweetbread in the beaten eggs followed by the flour mixture and toss to coat, shaking off any excess.

Deep fry sweetbreads for 3 to 5 minutes or until golden brown. Drain on paper towels quickly transfer onto a baking sheet lined with a cooling rack.

Season with salt and pepper and serve with honey-mustard dipping sauce.

31. Golden Brown Sweetbreads with Fennel Salad

Ingredients:

1 sprig thyme
1 tbsp whole black peppercorns
1 bay leaf
2 x 250 g veal sweetbreads
60 g shelled hazelnuts
1 large handful fresh white breadcrumbs
seasoned plain flour, to dust
1 egg, beaten
rapeseed or groundnut oil

Fennel salad:

2 bulbs fennel, finely sliced
16 radishes, finely sliced
1 handful blanched, toasted hazelnuts, roughly chopped
Mustard Salad Dressing
Watercress or other salad leaves, to garnish

Method:

Pour 500ml of water in a saucepan, then drop in the thyme, peppercorns, the bay leaf and a good pinch of salt. Bring to a boil then simmer for 2 minutes to bring out the flavours in the aromatics.

Add the sweetbreads and simmer gently for about 6 minutes.

Remove the sweetbreads from the liquid with a slotted spoon and allow to cool by refreshing them in iced water so you can handle them.

To make the hazelnut crumbs put the hazelnuts in a blender and blend until you reach a breadcrumb consistency. Mix the hazelnuts with the breadcrumbs and season with salt and pepper.

When the sweetbreads are cool enough to handle, remove the outer membrane along with any lumps of fat, sinews or veins. Slice the sweetbreads. Dust the sweetbreads in the seasoned flour, shake off any excess, then dip in the beaten egg. Allow any excess egg to drip off the sweetbreads, then cover in the hazelnut crumbs.

For the fennel salad: mix together the sliced fennel, radishes and chopped hazelnuts and season with salt and pepper.

Drizzle with a little of the dressing, taste and adjust seasoning as necessary.

When ready to serve, heat enough rapeseed or groundnut oil to shallow fry in a heavy-based frying pan, then fry the sweetbreads in the pan for 2 minutes on each side, making sure that both sides are golden and crisp. Remove and drain on kitchen paper. Serve immediately with the fennel salad, garnished with some green salad leaves.

32. Lancashire Tripe And Onions

Ingredients:

450 g (1 lb) dressed tripe, washed
3 medium onions, skinned and sliced
568 ml (1 pint) fresh milk
pinch of grated nutmeg
1 bay leaf (optional)
salt and pepper
25 g (1 oz) butter
45 ml (3 tbsp) plain flour
chopped fresh parsley, to garnish

Method:

Put the tripe in a saucepan and cover with cold water. Bring to the boil, then drain and rinse under running cold water. Cut into 2.5 cm (1 inch) pieces.

Put the tripe, onions, milk, nutmeg, bay leaf (if using) and salt and pepper into the rinsed out pan. Bring to the boil, cover and simmer for about 2 hours, until tender. Strain off the liquid and reserve 600 ml (1 pint).

Melt the butter in a saucepan, stir in the flour and cook gently for 1 minute, stirring. Remove pan from the heat and gradually stir in the reserved cooking liquid. Bring to the boil and continue to cook, stirring, until the sauce thickens.

Add the tripe and onions and reheat. Adjust the seasoning and serve sprinkled with parsley.

33. Tripe Espana

Ingredients:

1.5 kg tripe
1 kg cow's snout
1 veal trotter
salt
200 ml wine vinegar
4 l water
100 gr salted pork fat
1 ham bone
2 black small puddings
2 regular chorizos
2 onions
1 head garlic
1 bay leaf
parsley
white pepper
1 tbsp flour
1 tbsp pimentón

Method:

Cut the tripe, snout and trotter into pieces and place in a container with vinegar and salt.

Then wash in several changes of water and transfer to a pan with half the water (2 litres).

Bring to the boil, and discard the water. Cover again with water and add the pork fat, ham bone, chopped black pudding and chorizo, finely-chopped onion and garlic, bay leaf, parsley, salt and pepper. Bring to the boil and skim.

Lower the heat and simmer for about three hours.

In a frying-pan, make a sofrito with olive oil, a chopped onion, pimentón and flour.

Add this mixture to the tripe and boil everything together for 15 minutes.

Serve

34. Maxed Out Tripe

Ingredients:

300g chickpeas, soaked in water overnight
1kg clean tripe, cut into small bite size pieces
1 medium tomato, roughly chopped
1 (100g) bunch mint, tied in a bundle at the middle
4 garlic cloves, finely chopped
1 large onion, finely chopped
1 small pig's trotter cut into quarters, (half a trotter if large)
1 heaped tablespoon paprika (for colouring)
4 whole black peppercorns
1cm square fresh hot chili
300ml white wine of your choice
6 turns with the pepper grinder
salt to taste
1 (80g to 100g) chorizo, cut into thick slices (around 1.5cm to 2cm.)
80g to 100g black pudding, cut into thick slices (around 1.5cm. to 2cm.)
1 fresh mint sprig for each plate to garnish

Method:

Drain and rinse the chickpeas with clean water before adding them to a large pot.

To the pot add the tripe, tomato, mint bundle, garlic, onion, pig's trotter, paprika, peppercorns, chili and wine.

Pour water into the pot to cover. Add pepper and salt to taste.

Place the lid on the pot. When boiling starts, cook for 70 minutes. Halfway through cooking give a small stir and top up the evaporated liquid with boiling water if necessary.

Once cooking is done and the chickpeas and tripe are tender, add the chorizo and black pudding, then cook for an extra 3 minutes.
Remove and dispose the mint from the pot.
Serve tripe dish garnished with a sprig of fresh mint.

35. Simple Pig's Trotters

Ingredients:

2 salted pig's trotters, halved lengthways and soaked for 12 hours in a few changes of cold water

For the stock:
1 medium onion, left whole
1 small carrot
1 small leek, trimmed and washed
1 small parsnip
1 branch celery with leaves on
1 bouquet garni (thyme and laurel)
Plain flour for dipping the trotters in

For the sauce:
6-7 tablespoons extra virgin olive oil
1 small onion, finely chopped
1 clove garlic, finely chopped
1-2 sprigs parsley, most of the bottom stalk discarded, then finely chopped
4 tablespoons vegetable stock
200-250ml whole milk
3 tablespoons caster sugar

Drain the trotters and pat them dry. Singe over a gas flame and rinse under cold water. Place in a large pot.

Add the vegetables to the pot together with the bouquet garni. Cover well with water and place over a medium heat. As the water comes to the boil, skim it clean. Then lower the heat and simmer for 1½-2 hours or until the trotters are done. Don't add any salt to the cooking broth. The trotters will still be slightly salted.

Lift the cooked trotters out of the stock with a slotted spoon. Carefully take the largest bone out of each half, pat them slightly dry, then dip them in flour and set aside.

Put the oil in a large sauté pan and place over a medium heat. When the oil is hot, fry the trotters on both sides until lightly golden.

Transfer to a dish. Add the chopped onion to the oil and cook, stirring occasionally, until soft and
transparent. Add the garlic and parsley and cook until the onion and garlic are golden and the parsley crisp.

Reduce the heat to low. Add the stock and let it bubble for a minute or so before adding the milk and sugar. When the milk starts bubbling, drop in the cooked trotters and simmer, covered, for 20-30 minutes or until the sauce has thickened and the meat is very hot. If you think that the sauce is not thick enough, stir in a little flour and simmer for 5 more minutes.

Serve immediately.

36. Pork Trotter Terrine with Gribiche Sauce

Ingredients:

For the Terrine:
5 pounds (2 large or 3 medium) fresh trotters, including the hocks
1 large leek, de-stemmed and washed for dirt
1 large onion, peeled and washed for dirt
2 large or 3 medium carrots, peeled and washed
Salt
2 bay leaves
1 teaspoon black peppercorns
A small bunch of thyme tied together, or 1/2 teaspoon dried thyme
1 head garlic, split horizontally in half
2 tablespoons unsalted butter
1 cup minced shallots
1/4 cup Dijon mustard
Freshly ground black pepper
1 tablespoon plus 1 teaspoon chopped Italian parsley
A few tablespoons of all-purpose flour
1/2 cup panko crumbs

For the Sauce Gribiche:
1 tablespoon red wine vinegar
1/2 cup extra virgin olive oil
1 teaspoon Dijon mustard
2 teaspoons each chopped hard-cooked egg white and egg yolk
1 tablespoon minced non pareil capers, preferably Spanish
2 tablespoons minced tarragon
2 teaspoons minced chives
2 teaspoons minced chervil
1 tablespoon minced cornichons
2 teaspoons minced Italian parsley
1/4 teaspoon kosher salt
1/4 teaspoon coarse black ground pepper

Method:

Place the hocks in a large stockpot and add water to cover. Place the pot over high heat and bring to a boil, skimming away the foam that rises to the surface. Reduce the heat and simmer for 5 minutes to remove all the impurities.

Remove the hocks from the pot, discard the liquid, and rinse out the pot. Return the hocks to the pot and cover with cold water. Place the pot over high heat and bring to a simmer.

Add the leek, onion, carrots, 1 tablespoon of salt, bay leaves, peppercorns, thyme, and garlic and return the water to a simmer. Simmer for 2 to 3 hours, until the fat on the hocks is completely softened and the meat is tender and pulling away from the bone. Turn off the heat and leave the hocks in the liquid.

Meanwhile, sweat the shallots: Melt the butter in a large sauté pan over medium heat. Add the shallots and cook for about 2 minutes to soften them. Stir in 1 teaspoon of salt and remove from the heat.

Lift the hocks from the liquid and set in a bowl or baking sheet. While they are still hot but not scalding, use your fingers or a fork to separate the meat from the skin and fat, reserving the skin. Pull the meat apart, and set aside the bones for additional simmering in the stock.

Place the meat in a large bowl and keep in a warm spot. Scrape the fat from the skin and discard the fat. Finely chop the skin and stir it into the meat.

To shape the terrine: Cut two sheets of heavy duty foil, or layer several sheets of regular foil. Spoon half of the mixture onto one sheet, shaping it so that it is approximately 10 inches long and 2 inches in diameter. Roll the log up into the foil. Squeeze and twist the ends to compress the meat so that it is 8 to 10 inches long and 2 to 2 1/2 inches in diameter. This mixture will make 2 terrines.

Alternately, use cookie cutters or other circular rings to make individual terrines of trotters.
Refrigerate overnight. You will have approximately 10 to 12 servings.

For the Sauce Gribiche: Combine all the ingredients in a bowl, adding them in the order given. Let the sauce sit for at least 30 minutes, or refrigerate for up to a day. You will have about one cup.

To finish: Preheat the oven to 200/ 400F. Depending on how many servings you need, cut each serving into a 1 1/2 inch slice. Season both sides with salt and pepper and dip in flour; the flour should come up the sides of each slice. Spread a thin layer of Dijon mustard over the flour, and then dip into the panko crumbs to coat. At this point, the slices may be refrigerated for up to 30 minutes, or cooked immediately.

Heat a few tablespoons of oil or butter in a non-stick, oven proof skillet such as cast iron. When the pan is hot, carefully add the slices and let brown for about 30 seconds on the bottom side. Since they spatter as they cook, they will be finished in the oven.

Place the skillet in the oven for about 4 minutes to brown the top side. Be careful not to cook it for too long, or the trotters will break up. Remove the skillet from the oven and drain the trotters on paper towels, if needed.

To serve, place 2 tablespoons of the Sauce Gribiche on each serving plate to accompany the trotters.

37. Goats Trotters Curry

Ingredients:

5-6 goats trotters (Ask the butchers to chop them in half or smaller chunks that will fit in your saucepan)
2 bay leaves
6-7 black peppercorns
3 tbsp vegetable oil
2 small onions finely chopped
2 green chillies
8-9 cloves of garlic
2" piece of ginger
1 ½ tsp kashmiri chilli powder (or a mild paprika powder would be a good option)
4 tbsp whisked yoghurt
Salt to taste
2 tbsp roughly chopped coriander
2 tbsp roughly chopped mint
Juice of 1 lemon

For the paste:

2 tbsp coriander seeds
1 tbsp sesame seeds
100gms freshly grated coconut (or you can use desiccated)
5-7 green cardamom pods
4-5 black pepper corns
5 cloves

Method:

In a stock pot add all the cleaned and cut trotters along with the bay leaves and peppercorns. Add water covering all the trotters. Bring to a boil and simmer gently for 3 hours.

For the paste, add all the ingredients to a frying pan and dry roast the spices on medium heat. Stir them around for 2-3 minutes until you can see the colour start to change. Turn the heat off and let them cool slightly.

Now tip them into a coffee blender grinding to form a coarse powder. Set aside. Blend the ginger & garlic to a fine paste too with a little water and set aside.

Once the trotters have been boiling for 3 hours turn the heat off. Strain the stock and put the trotters aside. At this stage the trotters might be slightly gelatinous & sticky which means it needs a bit more cooking time along with the spices in the gravy.

Heat oil in a large heavy based sauce pan. Add the onions along with the green chillies. Fry the onions & let the chillies infuse their flavour in the oil. Soften the onions on medium heat for 5 minutes. Now add the ginger and garlic paste.

Stir well cooking out the raw flavour for a further 3 minutes. Tip in the paste and fry mixing well for 5-7 minutes until you see the oil leave the sides of the pan. Add the chili powder and stir. Lower the heat and add in the yoghurt a tablespoon at a time. Stir well to make sure it doesn't curdle but enhances the flavours to form a rich gravy with all the spices.

Add the trotters to the gravy and put the heat back to medium, coating all the pieces in the spice mix for 2-3 minutes. Ladle in most of the stock and bring the curry to a boil. (Leave a couple of ladles of the stock aside for later)

Simmer gently for a further hour. Make sure to stir it every 15 minutes or so just so it doesn't stick to the bottom of the pan. If you find the gravy is too thick you can add a little more of the left over stock. Season with salt and juice of a lemon.

To serve garnish with lots of fresh coriander & mint.

38. Ye Olde Jellied Pigs Feet

Ingredients:

4 lbs pigs trotters (whole)
1 washed whole onion, cut in half (with skin)
2 washed carrots, whole
2 whole, washed celery stalk
3 medium size garlic cloves, smashed flat using the flat end of a butter knife.
1 tablespoon salt
3 cups chicken broth
1 tablespoon sweet Hungarian Paprika
1 teaspoon fresh ground black pepper
Water, enough to cover.

Method:

Darken (Sear) skin of pig's feet by holding them over a flame or use a butane torch. Wash them very well in warm water, then place them in a pot, adding the chicken broth and enough water to cover well.

Bring to a boil and skim off froth (foam) rising to top. Lower heat and simmer slowly. Add the garlic, salt, black pepper, onion, carrot, celery and paprika, slow boil until meat falls apart from the bones, adding more water as needed to keep up the liquid level (about 5 or 6 hours), strain and pour liquid into a large glass baking dish or tin foil pan, then re-add only the meat pieces.

Refrigerator overnight to jell. Spoon into dinner soup plates and serve cold.

Before serving sprinkle with paprika.

Serves 4-5

39. Stornoway Style Black Pudding

Ingredients:

4 cups fresh pig's blood
2 1/2 teaspoons salt
1 1/2 cups steel-cut (pinhead) oatmeal
2 cups finely diced pork fat (or beef suet), finely chopped
1 large yellow onion, finely chopped
1 cup milk
1 1/2 teaspoons freshly ground black pepper
1 teaspoon ground allspice

Method:

Preheat the oven to 190C / 325F and grease 2 glass loaf pans. Stir 1 teaspoon of salt into the blood.

Bring 2 1/2 cups water to a boil and stir in the oats. Simmer, stirring occasionally, for 15 minutes, until just tender, not mushy.

Pour the blood through a fine sieve into a large bowl to remove any lumps. Stir in the fat, onion, milk, pepper, allspice and remaining 1 1/2 teaspoons salt. Add the oatmeal and mix to combine. Divide the mixture between the loaf pans, cover with foil, and bake for 1 hour, until firm. Cool completely. Seal in plastic wrap and wither freeze for extended use or store in the refrigerator for up to a week.

To serve, cut a slice about 1/2-inch thick off the loaf. Fry in butter or oil until the edges are slightly crisped and browned.

40. Sanguinaccio Dolce (Sweet Blood Pudding)

Ingredients:

1 litre pig's blood
1 liter milk
1 kg. sugar
100 grams almonds
100 grams hazelnuts
300 grams chocolate
cinnamon stick
ground cloves

Method:

Put the milk in a casserole dish and add the blood after it has been passed through a sieve.

Add the cinnamon and cloves, slowly add the sugar a little at a time to avoid forming lumps.

Place the casserole dish on the stove and heat until it thickens to the consistency of cream, gradually incorporating the chocolate, almonds and hazelnuts (all chopped very fine).

Pour into serving dishes and serve cold

41. Scandinavian Pig's Blood Rye Bread

Ingredients:

500 milliliters milk
60 grams yeast
100 grams butter
1 small red onion, diced
1.25 kilograms rye flour
1 kilogram bread flour
1 teaspoon salt
200 grams pig's blood
1 teaspoon sugar
500 milliliters molasses

Method:

Preheat the oven to 190C / 375F. Warm the milk. Add the yeast and allow the yeast to bloom for 10 minutes.

Meanwhile, put the butter in a pan over a medium heat and sauté the onion. Remove the sautéed onion from the heat and allow it to cool to room temperature.

Put the bloomed yeast in the bowl of standing mixer. Add the rye flour, bread flour, and salt and start to bring the dough together with a dough hook. Add the pig's blood, sugar, molasses, and onion.

Mix the dough until it becomes smooth. Allow the dough to double for 20 minutes. Divide the dough into 8 loaves. Poke the loaves with a fork all over.

Proof for 5 more minutes. Egg wash and bake for 20 minutes.

42. Crispy Lambs' Brains

Ingredients:

6 lambs' brains
Chicken stock
½ cup seasoned flour
2 eggs, beaten
1 cup fresh breadcrumbs or ready-made panko crumbs
Lard or olive oil

Method:

Place the lambs' brains in a pot and pour in enough cold chicken stock to cover.

Bring to the boil and simmer for 2 minutes before covering with a lid, turning off the heat and leaving to cool.

Once it's cool, remove from the liquid and dry with a paper towel. Trim off any bits of fat or tissue and separate the brains in half so you have 12 individual pieces that are about the size of a large mussel.

Dip each piece in flour, then egg and finally breadcrumbs.

Place carefully on a plate and refrigerate for half an hour – if you have the time – so that the coating sets.

Deep-fry in melted lard or olive oil until crisp and golden. Serve on a bed of salad with lemon wedges to squeeze over.

43. Old Fashioned Beef Brain

Ingredients:
0.5-0.6kg beef brain
2 tablespoons butter
2 tablespoons vinegar
1-2 bay leafs
3-4 peppercorns
1/5 tablespoon pepper
1 slice onion
1/3 teaspoon salt
200-250g sour cream
50g flour

Method:

Put the brain into cold water and add 1 tablespoon of vinegar. Leave the brain within the water for one hour.

Very gently remove the membrane of the brain without removing it from the water. Once membrane is gone replace the water.

Make sure water covers the brain. Put salt, peppercorns, bay leaf and the rest vinegar and place it on heat. As soon as water starts boiling, reduce the heat and let it boil slowly for 20 min.

In the meantime chop the onion into small pieces ready for frying.

Remove the boiled brain and put it on the colander for 3-5 min. When the moisture is almost gone, cut the brain into medium size pieces about 3-4 cm each.

Add flour to the brain and fry it in butter with onion, black pepper and any spices you like.

Once brain is ready, (has light brown color), add sour cream and cook it in the oven for 20-30 min. I use pyrex pan for this step. Serve it warm with fresh or cooked vegetables.

44. Sheep's Brains en Matelote

Ingredients:

6 sheep or lambs' brains
vinegar
sea salt
3 slices of bacon
1 small onion
2 cloves
1 small bunch of parsley
stock
bread for frying into croûtons
1 tbsp lemon juice

Method:

Place the brains in a pan of warm water. Remove the outer membranes and set aside to soak for 2 hours.

After this time, season a pan of boiling water with vinegar and salt. Add the brains and cook for about 30 minutes, or until quite firm.

Remove with a slotted spoon and plunge in cold water to prevent any further cooking. Add the bacon to a pan then add the brains, the onion (stuck with the 2 cloves), the parsley and a generous seasoning of salt and black pepper.

Pour over enough stock to cover then bring to a boil and cook for 25 minutes. In the meantime, fry some bread croûtons. Arrange the brains on a dish alternately with piles of bread croûtons then whisk the lemon juice into the matelote sauce, pour over the brains and croûtons then serve.

45. Sister Mary's Rooster Combs and Testicles.

Ingredients:

500g Rooster Combs and testicles
125 ml gin
80 ml water
6 slices ginger
7 tbsp soja sauce
20 g palm sugar
1 chilies
2 tbsp oyster sauce
2 tbsp Hoisin sauce
2 star anise
1 small piece of cinnamon stick

Method:

Place all the ingredients in a large saucepan and bring to the boil.

Cook covered for 10 minutes. Remove the lid and reduce sauce shaking it frequently until the meat is well coated.

Serve hot and garnish with the green onions and sesame seeds.

46. Pig's Ears with Sofrito

Ingredients:

2 pig's ears
1 onion, sliced
1 leek, cut into chunky slices
2 carrots, coarsely chopped
2 bay leaves
sea salt and black peppercorns

Sofrito:

1 tablespoon extra virgin olive oil
1 onion, finely diced
2 garlic cloves, finely diced
6 tablespoons white wine
1 teaspoon Spanish smoked paprika (hot)

Method:

First, cook the pig's ears. Simply put everything in a saucepan and cover with water. Boil for 2 hours, topping off with water if necessary and removing any foam that comes to the surface. Keep simmering until you can stick a knife into the thickest part of the ear very easily. Let the ears cool, then use a pair of scissors to cut them up into 3/4 in. squares.

For the sofrito, heat the oil in a frying pan and sauté the onion until soft but not colored. Make a paste with the garlic cloves and the wine in a pestle and mortar. Stir this into the onions along with the paprika, then add the chopped-up pig's ears.

Simmer until the wine has evaporated and you are left with sauce coating on the pork.

Eat as a snack or a tapas dish.

47. Zuppa di Polmone (Lung Soup)

Ingredients:

1 1/8 pound (500 g) veal lung
4 tablespoons rendered lard
1 medium onion, minced
1 tablespoon flour
1 tablespoon red wine vinegar
Salt and pepper to taste
1 quart (1 liter) boiling water
Toasted bread

Method:

Soak the lung in salted water for 3 hours. Rinse it well and boil it for 15 minutes in salted water. Drain it and dice it.

Heat the lard in a pot and sauté the onion for a few minutes, or until it turns golden. Add the lung and continue sautéing, stirring often for about 15 minutes. Add the flour, vinegar, a little salt and a generous grind of pepper, and mix well.

Add sufficient water to make a soup of it and simmer the soup for about 40 minutes.

Serve over toasted bread.

48. Slow Roasted Marrow Bones

Ingredients:

8 to 12 center-cut beef or veal marrow bones, 3 inches long, 3 to 4 pounds total
1 cup roughly chopped fresh parsley
2 shallots, thinly sliced
2 teaspoons capers
1 1/2 tablespoons extra virgin olive oil
2 teaspoons fresh lemon juice
Coarse sea salt to taste

Method:

Preheat oven to 230C / 450F degrees.

Put bones, cut side up, on foil-lined baking sheet or in ovenproof skillet.

Cook until marrow is soft and has begun to separate from the bone, about 15 minutes. (Stop before marrow begins to drizzle out.)

Meanwhile, combine parsley, shallots and capers in small bowl. Just before bones are ready, whisk together olive oil and lemon juice and drizzle dressing over parsley mixture until leaves are just coated.

Put roasted bones, parsley salad, salt and toast on a large plate. To serve, scoop out marrow, spread on toast, sprinkle with salt and top with parsley salad.

49. The Ultimate Rocky Mountain Oysters Recipe

Ingredients:

2 pounds bull testicles
1/2 cup granulated sugar
3/4 cup kosher salt
8 cups cold water
Milk
1 heaping tablespoon white vinegar
Salt and ground black pepper, to taste
1 cup all-purpose flour
1/4 cup cornmeal
Garlic powder to taste
1 cup milk
1 cup dry red wine
Louisiana hot sauce to taste
Peanut oil for frying

Method:

With a very sharp knife, split the tough skin-like muscle that surrounds each testicle ("oyster") Remove the skin.

In a large bowl or pot, dissolve 1/2 cup sugar and 3/4 cup kosher salt in 8 cups cold of water (water should cover the "oysters"); add the oysters; cover and let set for 1 hour.

Drain and rinse under cool water. Place "oysters" back into the bowl or pot (which has been rinsed clean) and pour enough milk over them to cover. Cover the bowl and let set for another hour. Drain and rinse well under cool water. These two steps help to draw the blood out. The milk-soak also helps to draw out the saltiness.

Transfer "oysters" to a large pot. Add the vinegar and enough cold water to cover "oysters". Bring to a boil. Reduce heat immediately and simmer for about 6 minutes. Drain again and plunge the cooked "oysters" into large bowl of ice water. Let stand until cool.

Slice each "oyster" into 1/4 to 1/3-inch thick ovals. Sprinkle with salt and pepper on both sides to taste.

Place the milk in a shallow bowl. Mix the wine and hot sauce to taste in a shallow bowl. In another shallow bowl, combine the flour, cornmeal and garlic powder to taste in a shallow bowl.

Dredge each "oyster" slice in the flour mixture. Dip into milk, then into the flour mixture. Dip into the wine mixture quickly. (Repeat procedure if a thicker crust is desired).

Fry oysters in hot oil until golden on both sides, being careful not to overcook the "oysters", since the longer they cook the tougher they become. Serve hot.

50. Mother's Haggis

Ingredients.

1 sheep's pluck. i.e. the animals heart, liver, and lungs..
Cold water.
1 sheep's stomach (empty).
1lb lightly toasted pinhead oatmeal (medium or coarse oatmeal).
1-2 tablespoons salt.
1 level tablespoon freshly ground black pepper.
1 tablespoon freshly ground allspice.
1 level tablespoon of mixed herbs.
8oz finely chopped suet.
4 large onions, finely chopped.
(lemon juice (or a good vinegar) is sometimes added as well as other flavourings such as cayenne pepper)

Method:

Wash the stomach in cold water until it is thoroughly clean and then soak it in cold salted water for about 8-10 hours.

Place the pluck in a large pot and cover with cold water. The windpipe ought to be hung over the side of the pot with a container beneath it in order to collect any drips. Gently simmer the pluck for approximately 2 hours or until it is tender and then leave the pluck to cool.

Finely chop or mince the pluck meat and then mix it with the oatmeal. Add about half a pint of the liquor in which the pluck was cooked (or use a good stock). Add the seasonings, suet and onions, ensuring everything is well mixed.

Fill the stomach with the mixture, leaving enough room for the oatmeal to expand into. Press out the air and then sew up the haggis. Prick the haggis a few times with a fine needle. Place the haggis it in boiling water and simmer for approximately 3 hours.
Serve with boiled or mashed potatoes and turnip. (Neeps and Tatties)

Printed in Great Britain
by Amazon

40412294R00046